Published by Angelis Publications
ISBN: 978-1-912484-30-0
www.angelispublications.com
© Angelis Publications 2019
All rights reserved

# Welcome

| Date | Name | Address / Email |
|------|------|-----------------|
|      |      |                 |

# Comments

| Date | Name | Address / Email |
| --- | --- | --- |
|  |  |  |

# Comments

| Date | Name | Address / Email |
|------|------|-----------------|
|      |      |                 |
|      |      |                 |
|      |      |                 |
|      |      |                 |
|      |      |                 |
|      |      |                 |
|      |      |                 |
|      |      |                 |
|      |      |                 |
|      |      |                 |
|      |      |                 |
|      |      |                 |
|      |      |                 |
|      |      |                 |
|      |      |                 |
|      |      |                 |

## Comments

| Date | Name | Address / Email |
|------|------|-----------------|
|      |      |                 |
|      |      |                 |
|      |      |                 |
|      |      |                 |
|      |      |                 |
|      |      |                 |
|      |      |                 |
|      |      |                 |
|      |      |                 |
|      |      |                 |
|      |      |                 |
|      |      |                 |
|      |      |                 |
|      |      |                 |
|      |      |                 |
|      |      |                 |

# Comments

| Date | Name | Address / Email |
|------|------|-----------------|
|      |      |                 |
|      |      |                 |
|      |      |                 |
|      |      |                 |
|      |      |                 |
|      |      |                 |
|      |      |                 |
|      |      |                 |
|      |      |                 |
|      |      |                 |
|      |      |                 |
|      |      |                 |
|      |      |                 |
|      |      |                 |
|      |      |                 |
|      |      |                 |

## Comments

| Date | Name | Address / Email |
|------|------|-----------------|
|      |      |                 |

# Comments

| Date | Name | Address / Email |
| --- | --- | --- |
| | | |

# Comments

| Date | Name | Address / Email |
|------|------|-----------------|
|      |      |                 |
|      |      |                 |
|      |      |                 |
|      |      |                 |
|      |      |                 |
|      |      |                 |
|      |      |                 |
|      |      |                 |
|      |      |                 |
|      |      |                 |
|      |      |                 |
|      |      |                 |
|      |      |                 |
|      |      |                 |
|      |      |                 |
|      |      |                 |
|      |      |                 |
|      |      |                 |

# Comments

| Date | Name | Address / Email |
|------|------|-----------------|
|      |      |                 |
|      |      |                 |
|      |      |                 |
|      |      |                 |
|      |      |                 |
|      |      |                 |
|      |      |                 |
|      |      |                 |
|      |      |                 |
|      |      |                 |
|      |      |                 |
|      |      |                 |
|      |      |                 |
|      |      |                 |
|      |      |                 |
|      |      |                 |

# Comments

| Date | Name | Address / Email |
|------|------|-----------------|
|      |      |                 |
|      |      |                 |
|      |      |                 |
|      |      |                 |
|      |      |                 |
|      |      |                 |
|      |      |                 |
|      |      |                 |
|      |      |                 |
|      |      |                 |
|      |      |                 |
|      |      |                 |
|      |      |                 |
|      |      |                 |
|      |      |                 |

## Comments

| Date | Name | Address / Email |
|------|------|-----------------|
|      |      |                 |
|      |      |                 |
|      |      |                 |
|      |      |                 |
|      |      |                 |
|      |      |                 |
|      |      |                 |
|      |      |                 |
|      |      |                 |
|      |      |                 |
|      |      |                 |
|      |      |                 |
|      |      |                 |
|      |      |                 |
|      |      |                 |
|      |      |                 |

# Comments

| Date | Name | Address / Email |
|------|------|-----------------|
|      |      |                 |
|      |      |                 |
|      |      |                 |
|      |      |                 |
|      |      |                 |
|      |      |                 |
|      |      |                 |
|      |      |                 |
|      |      |                 |
|      |      |                 |
|      |      |                 |
|      |      |                 |
|      |      |                 |
|      |      |                 |
|      |      |                 |
|      |      |                 |

# Comments

| Date | Name | Address / Email |
| --- | --- | --- |
|  |  |  |

# Comments

| Date | Name | Address / Email |
|------|------|-----------------|
|      |      |                 |
|      |      |                 |
|      |      |                 |
|      |      |                 |
|      |      |                 |
|      |      |                 |
|      |      |                 |
|      |      |                 |
|      |      |                 |
|      |      |                 |
|      |      |                 |
|      |      |                 |
|      |      |                 |
|      |      |                 |
|      |      |                 |

# Comments

| Date | Name | Address / Email |
|------|------|-----------------|
|      |      |                 |

## Comments

| Date | Name | Address / Email |
|------|------|-----------------|
|      |      |                 |
|      |      |                 |
|      |      |                 |
|      |      |                 |
|      |      |                 |
|      |      |                 |
|      |      |                 |
|      |      |                 |
|      |      |                 |
|      |      |                 |
|      |      |                 |
|      |      |                 |
|      |      |                 |
|      |      |                 |
|      |      |                 |
|      |      |                 |

## Comments

| Date | Name | Address / Email |
|------|------|-----------------|
|      |      |                 |

# Comments

| Date | Name | Address / Email |
|------|------|-----------------|
|      |      |                 |
|      |      |                 |
|      |      |                 |
|      |      |                 |
|      |      |                 |
|      |      |                 |
|      |      |                 |
|      |      |                 |
|      |      |                 |
|      |      |                 |
|      |      |                 |
|      |      |                 |
|      |      |                 |
|      |      |                 |
|      |      |                 |
|      |      |                 |

# Comments

| Date | Name | Address / Email |
|------|------|-----------------|
|      |      |                 |
|      |      |                 |
|      |      |                 |
|      |      |                 |
|      |      |                 |
|      |      |                 |
|      |      |                 |
|      |      |                 |
|      |      |                 |
|      |      |                 |
|      |      |                 |
|      |      |                 |
|      |      |                 |
|      |      |                 |
|      |      |                 |

# Comments

| Date | Name | Address / Email |
|------|------|-----------------|
|      |      |                 |
|      |      |                 |
|      |      |                 |
|      |      |                 |
|      |      |                 |
|      |      |                 |
|      |      |                 |
|      |      |                 |
|      |      |                 |
|      |      |                 |
|      |      |                 |
|      |      |                 |
|      |      |                 |
|      |      |                 |

# Comments

| Date | Name | Address / Email |
|------|------|-----------------|
|      |      |                 |
|      |      |                 |
|      |      |                 |
|      |      |                 |
|      |      |                 |
|      |      |                 |
|      |      |                 |
|      |      |                 |
|      |      |                 |
|      |      |                 |
|      |      |                 |
|      |      |                 |
|      |      |                 |
|      |      |                 |
|      |      |                 |

# Comments

| Date | Name | Address / Email |
|------|------|-----------------|
|      |      |                 |

# Comments

| Date | Name | Address / Email |
|------|------|-----------------|
|      |      |                 |
|      |      |                 |
|      |      |                 |
|      |      |                 |
|      |      |                 |
|      |      |                 |
|      |      |                 |
|      |      |                 |
|      |      |                 |
|      |      |                 |
|      |      |                 |
|      |      |                 |
|      |      |                 |
|      |      |                 |
|      |      |                 |

# Comments

| Date | Name | Address / Email |
|------|------|-----------------|
|      |      |                 |
|      |      |                 |
|      |      |                 |
|      |      |                 |
|      |      |                 |
|      |      |                 |
|      |      |                 |
|      |      |                 |
|      |      |                 |
|      |      |                 |
|      |      |                 |
|      |      |                 |
|      |      |                 |
|      |      |                 |
|      |      |                 |

# Comments

| Date | Name | Address / Email |
|------|------|-----------------|
|      |      |                 |
|      |      |                 |
|      |      |                 |
|      |      |                 |
|      |      |                 |
|      |      |                 |
|      |      |                 |
|      |      |                 |
|      |      |                 |
|      |      |                 |
|      |      |                 |
|      |      |                 |
|      |      |                 |
|      |      |                 |
|      |      |                 |

# Comments

| Date | Name | Address / Email |
|------|------|-----------------|
|      |      |                 |

## Comments

| Date | Name | Address / Email |
|------|------|-----------------|
|      |      |                 |
|      |      |                 |
|      |      |                 |
|      |      |                 |
|      |      |                 |
|      |      |                 |
|      |      |                 |
|      |      |                 |
|      |      |                 |
|      |      |                 |
|      |      |                 |
|      |      |                 |
|      |      |                 |
|      |      |                 |
|      |      |                 |

# Comments

| Date | Name | Address / Email |
|------|------|-----------------|
|      |      |                 |

## Comments

| Date | Name | Address / Email |
|------|------|-----------------|
|      |      |                 |
|      |      |                 |
|      |      |                 |
|      |      |                 |
|      |      |                 |
|      |      |                 |
|      |      |                 |
|      |      |                 |
|      |      |                 |
|      |      |                 |
|      |      |                 |
|      |      |                 |
|      |      |                 |
|      |      |                 |
|      |      |                 |

## Comments

| Date | Name | Address / Email |
|------|------|-----------------|
|      |      |                 |
|      |      |                 |
|      |      |                 |
|      |      |                 |
|      |      |                 |
|      |      |                 |
|      |      |                 |
|      |      |                 |
|      |      |                 |
|      |      |                 |
|      |      |                 |
|      |      |                 |
|      |      |                 |
|      |      |                 |
|      |      |                 |

# Comments

| Date | Name | Address / Email |
|------|------|-----------------|
|      |      |                 |

## Comments

| Date | Name | Address / Email |
|------|------|-----------------|
|      |      |                 |
|      |      |                 |
|      |      |                 |
|      |      |                 |
|      |      |                 |
|      |      |                 |
|      |      |                 |
|      |      |                 |
|      |      |                 |
|      |      |                 |
|      |      |                 |
|      |      |                 |
|      |      |                 |
|      |      |                 |
|      |      |                 |

# Comments

| Date | Name | Address / Email |
|------|------|-----------------|
|      |      |                 |

## Comments

| Date | Name | Address / Email |
|------|------|-----------------|
|      |      |                 |

# Comments

| Date | Name | Address / Email |
|------|------|-----------------|
|      |      |                 |
|      |      |                 |
|      |      |                 |
|      |      |                 |
|      |      |                 |
|      |      |                 |
|      |      |                 |
|      |      |                 |
|      |      |                 |
|      |      |                 |
|      |      |                 |
|      |      |                 |
|      |      |                 |
|      |      |                 |

# Comments

| Date | Name | Address / Email |
|------|------|-----------------|
|      |      |                 |
|      |      |                 |
|      |      |                 |
|      |      |                 |
|      |      |                 |
|      |      |                 |
|      |      |                 |
|      |      |                 |
|      |      |                 |
|      |      |                 |
|      |      |                 |
|      |      |                 |
|      |      |                 |
|      |      |                 |
|      |      |                 |

## Comments

| Date | Name | Address / Email |
|------|------|-----------------|
|      |      |                 |
|      |      |                 |
|      |      |                 |
|      |      |                 |
|      |      |                 |
|      |      |                 |
|      |      |                 |
|      |      |                 |
|      |      |                 |
|      |      |                 |
|      |      |                 |
|      |      |                 |
|      |      |                 |
|      |      |                 |
|      |      |                 |

# Comments

| Date | Name | Address / Email |
| --- | --- | --- |
|  |  |  |
|  |  |  |
|  |  |  |
|  |  |  |
|  |  |  |
|  |  |  |
|  |  |  |
|  |  |  |
|  |  |  |
|  |  |  |
|  |  |  |
|  |  |  |
|  |  |  |
|  |  |  |
|  |  |  |

# Comments

| Date | Name | Address / Email |
|------|------|-----------------|
|      |      |                 |
|      |      |                 |
|      |      |                 |
|      |      |                 |
|      |      |                 |
|      |      |                 |
|      |      |                 |
|      |      |                 |
|      |      |                 |
|      |      |                 |
|      |      |                 |
|      |      |                 |
|      |      |                 |
|      |      |                 |
|      |      |                 |

# Comments

| Date | Name | Address / Email |
|------|------|-----------------|
|      |      |                 |
|      |      |                 |
|      |      |                 |
|      |      |                 |
|      |      |                 |
|      |      |                 |
|      |      |                 |
|      |      |                 |
|      |      |                 |
|      |      |                 |
|      |      |                 |
|      |      |                 |
|      |      |                 |
|      |      |                 |
|      |      |                 |

## Comments

| Date | Name | Address / Email |
|------|------|-----------------|
|      |      |                 |
|      |      |                 |
|      |      |                 |
|      |      |                 |
|      |      |                 |
|      |      |                 |
|      |      |                 |
|      |      |                 |
|      |      |                 |
|      |      |                 |
|      |      |                 |
|      |      |                 |
|      |      |                 |
|      |      |                 |
|      |      |                 |

# Comments

| Date | Name | Address / Email |
|------|------|-----------------|
|      |      |                 |
|      |      |                 |
|      |      |                 |
|      |      |                 |
|      |      |                 |
|      |      |                 |
|      |      |                 |
|      |      |                 |
|      |      |                 |
|      |      |                 |
|      |      |                 |
|      |      |                 |
|      |      |                 |
|      |      |                 |
|      |      |                 |

# Comments

| Date | Name | Address / Email |
|------|------|-----------------|
|      |      |                 |
|      |      |                 |
|      |      |                 |
|      |      |                 |
|      |      |                 |
|      |      |                 |
|      |      |                 |
|      |      |                 |
|      |      |                 |
|      |      |                 |
|      |      |                 |
|      |      |                 |
|      |      |                 |
|      |      |                 |
|      |      |                 |

# Comments

| Date | Name | Address / Email |
|------|------|-----------------|
|      |      |                 |

# Comments

| Date | Name | Address / Email |
|------|------|-----------------|
|      |      |                 |

## Comments

| Date | Name | Address / Email |
|------|------|-----------------|
|      |      |                 |
|      |      |                 |
|      |      |                 |
|      |      |                 |
|      |      |                 |
|      |      |                 |
|      |      |                 |
|      |      |                 |
|      |      |                 |
|      |      |                 |
|      |      |                 |
|      |      |                 |
|      |      |                 |
|      |      |                 |
|      |      |                 |

# Comments

| Date | Name | Address / Email |
|------|------|-----------------|
|      |      |                 |
|      |      |                 |
|      |      |                 |
|      |      |                 |
|      |      |                 |
|      |      |                 |
|      |      |                 |
|      |      |                 |
|      |      |                 |
|      |      |                 |
|      |      |                 |
|      |      |                 |
|      |      |                 |
|      |      |                 |
|      |      |                 |

# Comments

| Date | Name | Address / Email |
|------|------|-----------------|
|      |      |                 |
|      |      |                 |
|      |      |                 |
|      |      |                 |
|      |      |                 |
|      |      |                 |
|      |      |                 |
|      |      |                 |
|      |      |                 |
|      |      |                 |
|      |      |                 |
|      |      |                 |
|      |      |                 |
|      |      |                 |
|      |      |                 |

# Comments

www.ingramcontent.com/pod-product-compliance
Lightning Source LLC
Chambersburg PA
CBHW060504240426
43661CB00007B/909